Hear

Written By
Lori Grant Kirk

TATE PUBLISHING & *Enterprises*

Heart for Jesus

This title is also available as a Tate Out Loud product. Visit www.tatepublishing.com for more information.

Published by Tate Publishing & Enterprises, LLC
127 E. Trade Center Terrace | Mustang, Oklahoma 73064 USA
1.888.361.9473 | www.tatepublishing.com

Tate Publishing is committed to excellence in the publishing industry. The company reflects the philosophy established by the founders, based on Psalm 68:11,
"The Lord gave the word and great was the company of those who published it."

Cover & Interior design by Leah LeFlore
Illustration by Kristen Polson

Published in the United States of America

ISBN: 978-1-60462-259-1
1. Youth & Children: Children: Non-Fic 2. Youth & Children: Children: Learnin
07.10.23

To my mother, for giving me the greatest gift of all … a heart for Jesus.

Halle Beth Trainor

This book belongs to

Asking Jesus in my heart
Means that I am saved.
It's not because I'm perfect,
Or that I'm well behaved.

JESUS
GLUE

It’s knowing Jesus died for me,
And took away my sin.
It’s making better choices
With the help from Him within.

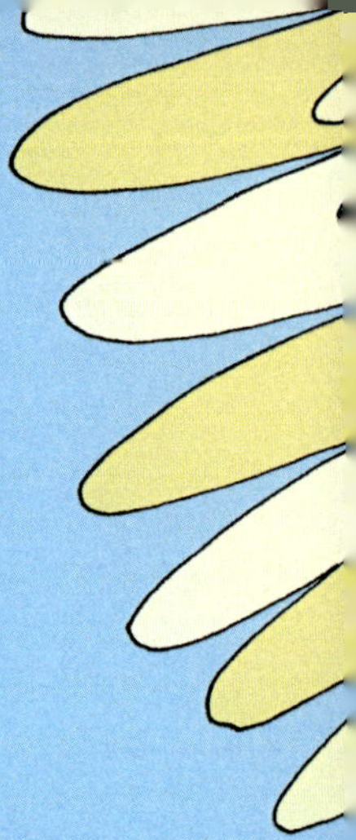

It’s nice to know there is a spot
In heaven just for me.
I will fly with angels
And sit on Jesus’ knee.

I talk to Jesus every day
To help me understand.
I want to make Him happy,
And do the best I can.

Jesus knows when I've been bad
Yet loves me anyway;
I always get another chance
Every single day!

So when I get confused
Or faced with something new,
I stop and ask myself,
What would Jesus do?

I know that Jesus never lied.
He knew how to share.
He treated others kindly,
With compassion and with care.

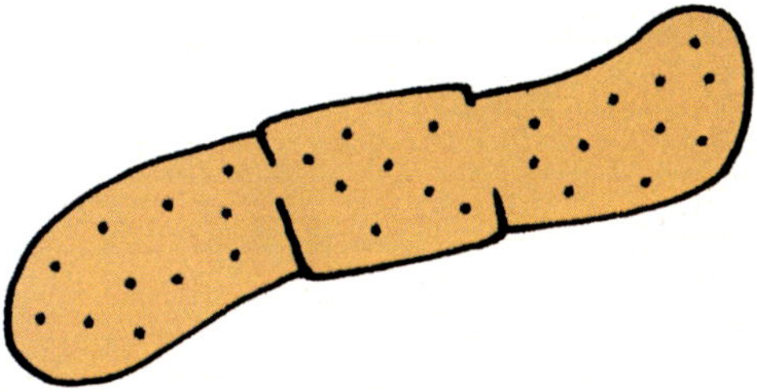

I can be like Jesus.
I can make Him proud.
I'll sing songs for Jesus,
And I'll sing them really loud!

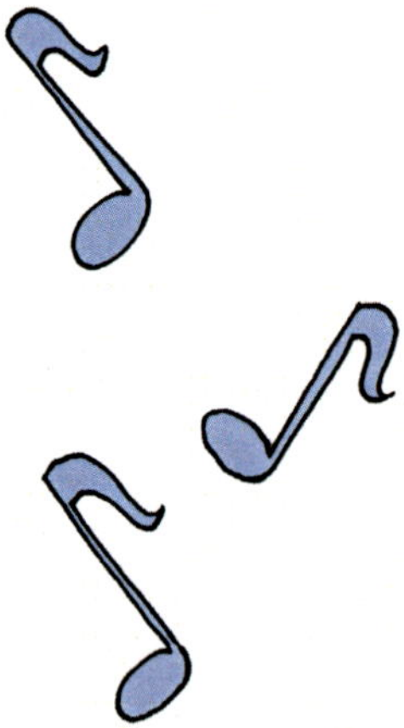

HYMNS

Some day I'll see Him face to face
In heaven up above.
For now I know my heart is filled
With His amazing love.

e|LIVE

listen|imagine|view|e ... ence

AUDIO BOOK DOWNLOAD I ... K!

In your hands you hold a complete digital enterta ... the paper
version of this book, this book includes a free dow ... ply
use the code listed below when visiting our websi ... ou
can listen to the book through your computer's spe ... file
to your portable music device (such as Apple's pop ...

How to get your free audio b ...

1. Visit www.tatepublishing.com and click on the e|LIVE logo on the home page.
2. Enter the following coupon code:
   841a-f9b1-7426-2388-770c-b2d5-9874-8d8a
3. Download the audio book from your e|LIVE digital locker and begin enjoying your new digital entertainment package today!